ALLOTMENTS TO CROW INDIANS

HEARING
BEFORE THE
COMMITTEE ON INDIAN AFFAIRS UNITED STATES SENATE
SIXTY-SIXTH CONGRESS.
FIRST SESSION
ON
S. 2890
A BILL TO PROVIDE FOR THE ALLOTMENT OF LANDS OF THE CROW TRIBE, FOR THE DISTRIBUTION OF TRIBAL FUNDS, AND FOR OTHER PURPOSES

SEPTEMBER 3, 1919

Printed for the use of the Committee on Indian Affairs

WASHINGTON
GOVERNMENT PRINTING OFFICE
1919

In the interest of creating a more extensive selection of rare historical book reprints, we have chosen to reproduce this title even though it may possibly have occasional imperfections such as missing and blurred pages, missing text, poor pictures, markings, dark backgrounds and other reproduction issues beyond our control. Because this work is culturally important, we have made it available as a part of our commitment to protecting, preserving and promoting the world's literature. Thank you for your understanding.

COMMITTEE ON INDIAN AFFAIRS.

CHARLES CURTIS, Kansas, *Chairman.*

ROBERT M. LA FOLLETTE, Wisconsin.
ASLE J. GRONNA, North Dakota.
ALBERT B. FALL, New Mexico.
BERT M. FERNALD, Maine.
CHARLES L. McNARY, Oregon.
SELDEN P. SPENCER, Missouri.
KNUTE NELSON, Minnesota.
MEDILL McCORMICK, Illinois.

HENRY F. ASHURST, Arizona.
ROBERT L. OWEN, Oklahoma.
EDWIN S. JOHNSON, South Dakota.
THOMAS J. WALSH, Montana.
JOHN B. KENDRICK, Wyoming.
ANDRIEUS A. JONES, New Mexico.
JOHN F. NUGENT, Idaho.

ALFRED B. CROSSLEY, *Clerk.*

ALLOTMENTS TO CROW INDIANS.

WEDNESDAY, SEPTEMBER 3, 1919.

United States Senate,
Committee on Indian Affairs,
Washington, D. C.

The committee met at 10.30 o'clock a. m., pursuant to call, in Room 226, Senate Office Building, Senator Charles Curtis presiding.

Present: Senators Curtis (chairman), Nelson, McNary, Johnson, Walsh of Montana, and McCormick; also the following delegates from the Crow Reservation: Frank Yarlott, John Frost, Thomas Medicine Horse, Sits Down Spotted, Mark Wolfe, Hartford Bear Claw, and Robert Yellowtail.

The committee had under consideration the following bill:

A BILL To provide for the allotment of lands of the Crow Tribe, for the distribution of tribal funds, and for other purposes.

Be it enacted by the Senate and House of Representatives of the United States of America in Congress assembled, That the Secretary of the Interior be, and he hereby is, authorized and directed to cause to be surveyed any unsurveyed lands within the Crow Indian Reservation in Montana, and thereafter to allot, as hereinafter provided, all such lands suitable for allotment not herein reserved, among the members of the Crow Tribe, as follows, namely, one hundred and sixty acres to every enrolled member, entitled to allotment, who died unallotted after December 31, 1905, and before the passage of this act; next, one hundred and sixty acres to every allotted member living at the date of the passage of this act, who may then be a head of a family and have not received allotment as such head of a family; and thereafter to pro rate the remaining unallotted allotable lands and allot them so that every enrolled member living on the date of the passage of the act and entitled to allotment shall receive in the aggregate an equal share of the allotable tribal lands for his total allotment of land of the Crow Tribe: *Provided,* That allotments made hereunder shall vest title in the allottee subject only to existing tribal leases, which leases in no event shall be renewed or extended by the Secretary of the Interior after the passage of this act, and shall be evidenced by patents in fee to competent Indians, but by trust patent to incompetent Indians, the force and legal effect of the trust patents to be as is prescribed by the general allotment act of February 8, 1887 (Twenty-fourth Statutes, page 388), as amended, and the election as to the kind of patent to be made by the competent allottee for himself and his minor children; but for the incompetent by the Secretary of the Interior: *Provided,* That priority of selection, up to three hundred and twenty acres, is hereby given to the members of the tribe who have as yet received no allotment on the Crow Reservation, and thereafter all members enrolled for allotment hereunder shall in all respects be entitled to equal rights and privileges, as far as possible, in regard to the time, manner, and amount of their respective selections.

Sec. 2. That the Secretary of the Interior shall, as speedily as possible, after the passage of this act, prepare a complete roll of the members of the Crow Tribe who died unallatted after December 31, 1905, and before the passage of this act; also, a complete roll of the allotted members of the tribe who at the date hereof are living and are heads of families but have not received full allotments as such; also, a complete roll of the unallotted members of the tribe living at the date hereof who are entitled to allotmnts. Such rolls when completed shall be deemed the final allotment rolls of the Crow Tribe, on which allotment of all tribal lands and distribution of all tribal funds existing at the date hereof shall be made. The rolls shall show the English, as well as the Indian, name of the allottee; the age, if living; the sex, whether declared competent or incompetent; the description or descriptions of the allotments; and any other fact deemed by the Secreary of he Interior necessary or proper.

SEC. 3. That any names found to be on the tribal rolls fraudulently may, upon request of the tribal council, at any time within three years from the passage of this act, be stricken therefrom by the Commissioner of Indian Affairs, with the approval of the Secretary of the Interior, after giving all parties in interest a full opportunity to be heard in regard thereto; and any allotment made to such fraudulent allottee shall be canceled and shall then be subject to disposition under the provisions of this act: *Provided*, That nothing herein contained shall be construed to deprive any such persons of the protection in the premises provided under existing law.

SEC. 4. That such of the unallotted lands as are now used for agency, school, or religious purposes shall remain reserved from allotment so long as such agency, school, or religious institutions, respectively, are maintained for the benefit of the tribe: *Provided*, That the Secretary of the Interior, upon the request of the tribal council, is hereby authorized and directed to cause to be issued a patent in fee to the duly authorized missionary board or other proper authority of any religious organization heretofore engaged in mission or school work on the reservation for such lands theren as have been heretfore set aside and are now occupied for such organizations for missionary or school purposes.

SEC. 5. That any and all minerals, including oil and gas, on any of the lands to be allotted hereunder are reserved for the benefit of the members of the tribe in common and may be leased under existing law for mineral purposes, under such rules, regulations, and conditions as the Secretary of the Interior may prescribe: *Provided, however*, That allotment hereunder may be made of lands classified as valuable chiefly for coal or other minerals and be patented as herein provided with a reservation, set forth in the patent, of the coal, oil, gas, or other mineral deposits for the benefit of the Crow Tribe: *And provided further*, That at the expiration of fifty years from the date of approval of this act the coal, oil, gas, or other mineral deposits upon or beneath the surface of said allotted lands shall become the property of the individual allottee or his heirs or assigns.

SEC. 6. That there is hereby appropriated the sum of $50,000, or so much thereof as may be necessary, for the purpose of making the surveys and allotments provided for herein, which sum, or so much thereof as may be expended for the purpose of carrying out the provisions of this act, shall be reimbursed to the United States from any funds in the Treasury belonging to said tribe.

SEC. 7. That any allotment, or part of allotment, provided for under this act, irrigable from any irrigation system now existing or hereafter constructed by the Government on the said reservation, shall bear its pro rata share, computed on a per-acre basis, of the cost of constructing such system: *Provided*, That no additional irrigation system shall be established or constructed on the Crow Reservation until the tribal consent thereto has been duly and legally obtained. All charges against allotments authorized by this section may be reimbursed in not less than ten annual payments, and the Secretary of the Interior may fix such operation and maintenance charges against such allotments as may be reasonable and just, to be paid as provided by law. Unless otherwise paid, these latter charges may, with the allottee's consent, be paid from or made a charge upon his individual share of the tribal fund, when said fund is available for distribution; and if any allottee shall receive patent in fee to his allotment before the amount so charged against his land has been paid, when such unpaid amount shall become and be a lien upon his allotment, and may may be enforced by the Secretary of the Interior by foreclosure as a mortgage; and should any Indian sell any part of his allotment, with the approval of the Secretary of the Interior, the amount of such unpaid charges against the land so sold shall be a first lien thereon, and may be enforced by the Secretary of the Interior by foreclosure as a mortgage; and delivery of water to such land may be refused, within the discretion of the Secretary of the Interior, until all dues are paid: *Provided*, That no right to water or to the use of any irrigation ditch or other structure on said reservation shall vest until the owner of the land to be irrigated shall comply with such rules and regulations as the Secretary of the Interior may prescribe, and he is hereby authorized to prescribe such rules and regulations as may be deemed reasonable and proper for making effective the foregoing provisions, and to refuse delivery of water to any tract of land until the owner thereof shall have complied therewith: *Provided, however,* That in no case shall any allottee be required to pay either construction, operation, or maintenance charges for such irrigation privileges, or any of them, until water has been actually delivered to his allotment and used by him, his heirs, or assigns thereon, or until delivery of water thereto or thereon has been requested by him in writing.

Sec. 8. That lands within said reservation, whether allotted, unallotted, or otherwise disposed of, shall be subject to all laws of the United States prohibiting the introduction of intoxicating liquors into the Indian country until otherwise provided by Congress.

Sec. 9. That any unallotted lands on the Crow Reservation chiefly valuable for the development of water power shall be reserved from allotment or other disposition hereunder, for the benefit of the Crow Tribe of Indians, and be held subject to such sale, lease, or other disposition as the tribe may, with the approval of Congress, hereafter make thereof.

Sec. 10. That jurisdiction be, and hereby is, conferred upon the Court of Claims, with right of appeal as in other cases to the Supreme Court of the United States, to hear, consider, and render final judgment in any and all claims that the Crow Tribe of Indians may have arising under treaty stipulation or agreement of the United States with the Crow Tribe or under any act of Congress relating to Indian affairs, or under any decision or ruling of any executive department of the United States, or which may be due to, or arise out of, any alleged failure, refusal, or neglect on the part of the United States in its capacity as trustee or guardian to hold, protect, preserve, and distribute, or pay over, to the tribe, any moneys lawfully due the tribe, with such interest thereon as may be provided by law. Any suit or suits hereunder shall be instituted by petition, with the Crow Tribe as party plaintiff and the United States as party defendant, such petition to be verified by the attorney or attorneys employed by the tribe to prosecute the claims: *Provided,* That the court may in the same suit also hear, consider, and adjudicate any claim that the United States may have against the tribe: *Provided further,* That upon final determination of any suit or suits hereunder the Court of Claims shall have jurisdiction to decree the fees or compensation to be paid to the attorney or attorneys employed by the tribe, and the same shall be paid out of any sum or sums found due therein.

Sec. 11. That so much of article 3 of the act of April 27, 1904, entitled "An act to ratify and amend an agreement with the Indians of the Crow Reservation in Montana, and making appropriations to carry the same into effect" (33 Stats., p. 352), as relates to the disposition of the trust funds of the tribe at the expiration of the fifteen-year period named in the act, to the purchase of cattle, to the distribution of cattle among the Indians of the reservation; to the purchase of jackasses, stallions, and ewes; to the building of fences; the erection of schoolhouses and hospitals; the purchase of additional cattle or sheep; the construction of ditches, dams, and canals; and to the establishment of a trust fund for the benefit of the Crow Indians thereunder, be, and the same is hereby, repealed, and the Secretary of the Interior is hereby authorized and directed to dispose of the existing tribal herd by distributing the cattle equally among the members of the tribe living at the date hereof and enrolled for allotment hereunder, and to distribute all tribal moneys available equally among the enrolled members of the tribe: *Provided,* That such members as are minors or incompetents and do not desire to have their distributive shares of cattle in kind may have their cattle sold under the direction of the Secretary of the Interior and the proceeds thereof placed to their credit, to be held or disposed of as other funds of individual members of the tribe under existing law: *Provided further,* That all remaining trust funds arising under the terms of the said agreement or otherwise, with such interest thereon as may now be due, shall be set aside and draw interest at the rate of 4 per centum per annum until the same are distributed as herein provided.

Sec. 12. That upon the approval of this act the Secretary of the Interior shall forthwith appoint a commission consisting of three persons to enroll the living members of the tribe and to divide them into two classes, competents and incompetents, said commission to be constituted as follows: One of said commissioners shall be an enrolled member of the Crow Indian Tribe and shall be selected by a majority vote of three delegates from each of the districts on the Crow Reservation; one commissioner shall be a legal resident of the State of Montana, and shall be selected by the Secretary of the Interior, on the recommendation of the duly constituted representatives of the Crow Tribe of Indians; and one commissioner shall be a representative of the Department of the Interior and shall be selected by the Secretary of the Interior. Said commission shall be governed by regulations prescribed by the Secretary of the Interior, and the classification of the members of the tribe hereunder shall be subject to his approval. That within thirty days after their appointment said commissioners shall meet at some point within the Crow Indian Reservation and organize by the election of one of their number as chairman. That said commissioners shall then proceed personally to classify the members as above indicated, including in the competent class all minors whose parents are competent Indians. Said commissioners shall be paid a salary of not to exceed $10 per day each, and necessary expenses while actually employed in the work of making this classification, exclusive of subsistence, to be approved by the Secretary of the Interior, such classification to be completed within six months from the date of organizing the commission.

SEC. 13. That every member of the Crow Tribe shall designate as a homestead land not to exceed 640 acres, already allotted or to be allotted hereunder, and such homestead shall remain inalienable for a period of twenty-five years from the date of issuance of patent therefor, or until the death of the allottee: *Provided*, That the Secretary of the Interior may extend the trust period on such homestead allotments of incompetent Indians in accordance with the provisions of existing law.

SEC. 14. That exchanges of allotments by and among the members of the tribe may be made under the supervision of the Secretary of the Interior with a view to enabling allottes to group their allotted lands on the Crow Reservation, but always with due regard for the value of the lands involved. And in cases where patents have already been issued for such allotments proper conveyance shall be made back to the United States by the allottee, whereupon the land shall become subject to disposition in the same manner as other lands under the provisions of this act.

The CHAIRMAN. The committee will come to order. Mr. Yellowtail, the committee desires to ask you a few questions.

STATEMENT OF ROBERT YELLOWTAIL, DELEGATE FROM THE CROW RESERVATION.

The CHAIRMAN. I want ask you a number of questions about this bill, and then have you go over the matter, and there are other members of the committee who may desire to do the same thing, and then when there is a quorum of the committee present, you may make your statement. Will you be willing to do that?

ROBERT YELLOWTAIL. Yes, sir; I am at the disposal of the committee.

The CHAIRMAN. In the first place, I want to know why you ask for the allotment of 160 acres to every enrolled member entitled to allotment, who died unallotted after December 31, 1905, and before the passage of this act? That means that you allot to every Indian who has died between 1905 and the passage of this act. What is the object of that?

ROBERT YELLOWTAIL. The object in inserting that in the bill was to take care of a number of children that were born after the rolls were closed by Mr. Rankin, and who had died since. Some of them had been recorded after their death and some before their death. There is a ruling of the department to the effect that those that have been recorded, that were recorded after their death, are not entitled to allotment. We have a lot of them who because of their ignorance or the negligence of their parents, I might say, as to the existence of any such rule, failed to have their children recorded at the agency office before their death, and the result is that they are not entitled to allotment, as I understand, under the existing regulation.

Now, this is to overcome any obstacle of that nature that might bob up to prevent the allotment of a child who because of the parents' fault would not be eligible to receive allotment. That is the thought we had in mind when we inserted that provision.

The CHAIRMAN. It has never been the practice to allot a dead Indian; as soon as an Indian dies his interest in the property reverts to the tribe.

ROBERT YELLOWTAIL. In this instance, the tribe is willing that they be allotted.

The CHAIRMAN. Where do you want the property to go, to his father or mother?

ROBERT YELLOWTAIL. It would naturally go to the heirs in such case, the father and mother.

The CHAIRMAN. It would descend under the laws of Montana.

ROBERT YELLOWTAIL. The assistant commissioner, Mr. Meritt, expressed the desire to take care of the matter at the conference we had with him at the Crow Agency.

Senator MCNARY. If a child dies without issue, does it go to the parent—the father?

Senator WALSH of Montana. The parent—the father.

Senator MCNARY. As tenants in common?

The CHAIRMAN. Now, in the first clause here you also provide for the allotment of fee patents to minors.

Senator WALSH of Montana. Before we pass from that, is that a departure, Mr. Meritt?

Mr. MERITT. Yes, sir.

The CHAIRMAN. It never has been done, has it?

Mr. MERITT. No, sir; but the Crow Indians have repeatedly requested that this action be taken, and inasmuch as it is the unanimous desire of the Crow Indians that the children who have died since the allotment rolls closed should have allotment, we have told them that we would not interpose any objection.

ROBERT YELLOWTAIL. Could you add that the Indians at the agency, in conference, when you were there a week or two ago, made a direct request of you for that?

Mr. MERITT. Yes, sir; the Indians have repeatedly requested that that action be taken.

The CHAIRMAN. Was there any object except that of giving the land to the parents? You see these Indians, if this allotment under this bill goes through, are going to have an awful acreage. Of course, they would have more if this bill should not pass.

Mr. MERITT. The Crow Indians have expressed a desire that this method be pursued in the distribution of their property.

Senator WALSH of Montana. About how many are there, Mr. Meritt?

Mr. MERITT. Probably 300, are there not?

ROBERT YELLOWTAIL. I doubt if there will be that many—well, that would cover every one. It would probably be under that figure.

Senator WALSH of Montana. It seems to me that that does not quite cover the matter. The bill says "who died unallotted after December 31, 1905."

Robert YELLOWTAIL. Of course this includes the allotted as well as the unallotted—the living as well as the dead.

Senator WALSH of Montana. But it does not say so.

Robert YELLOWTAIL. Well, "unallotted" is the word we used to cover both living and dead, because the living are unallotted also; they have no allotments as yet, and it would take another act.

Mr. MERITT. The children have taken tentative selections, but they have not been allotted.

Robert YELLOWTAIL. It means the living and the dead because the living and the dead have never received allotments.

The CHAIRMAN. Well, that can be taken care of by a proper amendment.

Are there any further questions upon this subject?

Senator WALSH of Montana. That is all, Mr. Chairman.

The CHAIRMAN. Now, you provide for patent in fee for minors, in line 19, page 2. Why do you want a patent in fee given a minor? It makes the property at once subject to sale and subject to taxation. If you insert that you would not have a minor with an acre of land when he arrived at age.

Robert YELLOWTAIL. We are willing to cut out the minor children.

Mr. MERITT. We object to that provision, Mr. Chairman.

Robert YELLOWTAIL. We consent to striking out the minor children. That will make it for all competent Indians. If the idea of the office, or the Indian Bureau, or the Government at large, you might say, is to as soon as possible let the Indians, as Senator Walsh has stated several times in the committee room, strike out for themselves and sink or swim—and which I think is the prevailing policy or idea with regard to the final emancipation of the Indians, if you may so call it—I think this provision comes in very properly with that in view. As fast as they deem an individual competent to take care of his own self, the prop should be let down and he should be allowed to strike out for himself.

Senator WALSH of Montana. I do not follow that exactly. The bill provides:

> That allotments made hereunder shall vest title in the allottee subject only to existing tribal leases, which leases in no event shall be renewed or extended by the Secretary of the Interior after the passage of this act, and shall be evidenced by patents in fee to competent Indians, but by trust patent to incompetent Indians, the force and legal effect of the trust patents to be as is prescribed by the general allotment act of February 8, 1887, as amended, and the election as to the kind of patent to be made by the competent allottee for himself and his minor children.

Now it provides——

Mr. MERITT. That whole provision should be stricken out, Mr. Chairman.

Senator WALSH of Montana. It provides above that the patent is to be in fee to the competent Indian, so he does not make any election at all; he gets the patent in fee, and the restricted patent goes to the incompetent Indian and he has nothing to choose in the matter.

Robert YELLOWTAIL. Yes; I see there is a conflict there.

Mr. MERITT. Mr. Chairman, I suggest that the language in lines 17, 18, and 19, after the words "as amended" be stricken out; that is, "and the election as to the kind of patent to be made by the competent allottee for himself and his minor children." Strike out all down to that point, beginning with line 17 and ending with line 19.

Senator WALSH of Montana. But that would give the Secretary of the Interior an opportunity to determine whether an incompetent Indian should have a trust patent or a patent in fee, but the incompetent should not have a patent in fee under any circumstances.

ROBERT YELLOWTAIL. That is provided for expressly in the language that follows here. There is no attempt here to give an incompetent Indian a fee patent anywhere.

Senator WALSH of Montana. That is the language here.

ROBERT YELLOWTAIL. It provides " for himself and his minor children." We are willing to exclude the children from that part of it, but I can not see, as to the competent Indian—if you are going to make him competent—why you should give him a trust patent if he does not want a trust patent. Mr. Meritt has suggested that that be stricken out.

Senator WALSH of Montana. It is already provided above as follows. " subject only to existing tribal leases, which leases in no event shall be renewed or extended by the Secretary of the Interior after the passage of this act, and shall be evidenced by patents in fee for competent Indians "——

The CHAIRMAN. And by trust patents.

Senator WALSH of Montana. And " by trust patents to incompetent Indians."

ROBERT YELLOWTAIL. Yes; you are right about that.

Mr. MERITT. If you strike out all after the words " as amended " in line 17, down to the word " provided " in line 20, it will meet the situation.

The CHAIRMAN. I thought I would suggest that we make notes as we go along, and I thought that I would talk with members of the committee and probably appoint a subcommittee to redraft this bill in connection with the office and with these men, so that we can cover all these points. I have been asking these questions because of what has occurred to me in the reading of the bill. I asked each member of the committee to read it.

ROBERT YELLOWTAIL. May I ask a question—I see the viewpoint. All the Indians that would be deemed competent are not here, and I want to ask if it is possible to insert a provision to give the competent Indians who might think otherwise, and who have not so expressed themselves in council—would it be in conflict with any existing regulations or any law to say to the competent Indians that they may elect, that they may give their election as to the kind of patent desired?

Senator WALSH of Montana. You can put it in above the word " evidenced," inserting the words " all competent Indians at their election shall have patents in fee or trust patents."

ROBERT YELLOWTAIL. That is possible, is it? That would be a provision we would like to insert. I am against forcing any kind of patent on any individual. If he wants a patent in trust and immediately thereafter requests the Secretary to issue a fee patent, I feel that that is his business, if the Secretary says it is all right. It is to prevent the possible making of any gypsy Indians at any time.

Senator MCNARY. If he is classified as competent, he still could have his choice as to a trust title or a patent in fee simple?

ROBERT YELLOWTAIL. Yes, sir.

Senator McNary. I see your position.

Robert Yellowtail. I would hesitate to say to a competent Indian, if there is any other way out of it, " you have to grab a fee patent and go on."

Senator Walsh of Montana. That is a good idea; that can be taken care of easily.

The Chairman. Yes; that can be easily taken care of.

Robert Yellowtail. How is that, Frank?

The Chairman. You may talk to him about that matter later, because we will want to go in a few minutes.

In section 2 you provide that " a complete roll of the allotted members of the tribe who at the date hereof are living," etc. Why would it not be better—and I am asking both yourself and the Assistant Commissioner—to fix a date in the future, say the 1st day of July or the 1st day of January, about the time you complete the roll, to have everybody enrolled up to that time?

If you do not do it, you are going to have the same situation as we had with the Iowas, I think, or the Otoes, I think, in Oklahoma, when we had certificates issued to a great many children who were born between the passage of the act and the allotment. Of course they thought they were entitled to the land and have been bothering Congressmen from that State and other States for years, wanting to know why certificates were issued to them and they never were given allotments. I do not see why certificates were given after the date of the passage of the act when the act provided that they should be allotted only up to the date of the passage of the act.

Senator Walsh of Montana. That is the change you suggest, " at the date hereof"?

The Chairman. Yes; make it to cover all children born on or before the 1st day of January, 1920. That would give you plenty of time. You can complete the roll in that time, can you not? Make it about the time you complete the roll and then you will get everybody on and nobody is going to have his certificate then and come up and bother you by reason of some mistake of some officer. I simply call that to your attention, because I know that did occur in Oklahoma in quite a number of cases.

Senator Walsh of Montana. I am quite sure it would be better to fix a definite date.

The Chairman. That is what I say, a definite date ahead.

Mr. Meritt. How about six months after date of passage of this act?

The Chairman. It ought to be about the time you are going to complete your rolls.

Senator Walsh of Montana. Make it six months after passage of this act, and if it is delayed in any way there ought to be still plenty of time.

The Chairman. You can talk that over with your people.

Now, in section 3 you provide for the elimination of fraudulent allottees three years. That is, it seems to me, clearly out of the question. In the meantime you would have all your land allotted and patents would be issued. These complaints ought to be filed within six months.

Robert Yellowtail. We are agreeable to that; we will agree to make that one year.

The CHAIRMAN. In the Osage we made it 90 days, did we not, Mr. Meritt?

Mr. MERITT. It was a short time.

The CHAIRMAN. Then you provide, too, for the tribal council. That is a pretty large body. In the Osage we provided that the principal chief should file the complaint. I wish you would think about that; it is one of the questions that will come up, and it is in my mind.

ROBERT YELLOWTAIL. In that connection, suppose these very lands that this provision aims at here, sold under fee patents, as in some cases they have been?

The CHAIRMAN. You could not reach that land under the laws of your State, could you Senator Walsh?

Senator WALSH of Montana. No, sir.

ROBERT YELLOWTAIL. Could not there be a provision inserted whereby the purchase price of the land may be recovered if proven they were not entitled to it and was fraudulent.

Senator WALSH of Montana. That could be done without any provision.

The CHAIRMAN. If they were fraudulent and if they had the money.

ROBERT YELLOWTAIL. That would necessarily follow.

The CHAIRMAN. Now, in section 4, you have made no arrangement for cemeteries or town sites. I do not know whether you want a town site on your reservation or not.

ROBERT YELLOWTAIL. That is a question I think we thrashed out with Senator Walsh last year or the year before, and we agreed to take that out of the bill. He didn't know why it was in there.

The CHAIRMAN. What is that, the town sites?

ROBERT YELLOWTAIL. Yes; the town sites.

The CHAIRMAN. Would it not be advisable to have a town site or two?

ROBERT YELLOWTAIL. It was during the time you had your sick spell and you called me up to your office. When you came to town sites you said you would be willing to see it go along with the military reservation. Do you not remember that? But, as for town sites, Senator Curtis, I think Superintendent Asbury will agree with me; here on this one creek alone we have got Wyola to begin with, 8 miles from the reservation line we have got Wyola. There is a little town site there at the natural place, the junction of Pass Creek and Little Horn River right here (indicating on map). You have a town site located there. I think they are selling lots there.

The CHAIRMAN. Who owns it?

ROBERT YELLOWTAIL. Black Hawk I think has an additon. He is adding to the town site. That is sufficient to take care of the development of this country I think for quite awhile to come. These are all hills——

Senator WALSH of Montana. I want to make this suggestion before I leave the committee, and you may talk about it. I had the strongest kind of appeals from the American Legion——

The CHAIRMAN. Soldiers?

Senator WALSH of Montana. Yes; who want an opportunity to homestead this land, or at least, as I understand the matter, have a preference in the disposition of them, and the matter has been agitated quite a good deal. I did not agree to do any more in the matter than to call it to the attention of the committee, and I mention it now, and I will ask you to consider it.

The CHAIRMAN. I had a telephone from the editor of the Soldiers' Magazine asking me the same question this morning, and I told him we probably only had a half an hour and we would not get very far, but that we would take that question up later.

Senator WALSH. I suppose you have heard about it, Robert.

ROBERT YELLOWTAIL. Oh, yes, sir; they told us they would send a delegate along with us, but he did not show up.

Senator WALSH. Mr. Peet was here 10 days ago; he is one of the officers of his legion, and that was a day or two before the 20th. I asked him to remain over and come before the committee and present their views about the matter, but he was called away.

The CHAIRMAN. We will present it to the committee when we meet again. It seems to me from the experience of other people on the other reservations, it would pay the tribe to set aside one or two sections in proper places for town sites; it would bring you very much more money; it would be something that would be brought in right away. You could put a provision in that it was not to be taxed until it was sold; you could have the regular sale and probably sell nearly all of it at one sale. That has been done on several reservations and why not give your tribe the benefit of the profit you are going to derive out of a town site rather than to give it to some individual who would be the fortunate man—giving him an allotment which would bring him $100,000 while others will get an allotment which will bring only a few thousand?

ROBERT YELLOWTAIL. I know the reservation a little bit better than you do, Senator, and I am trying to tell you——

The CHAIRMAN. That is why I am asking the question.

ROBERT YELLOWTAIL. Every place on the reservation that is adaptable and suitable for a town site, has a town site on it right now, and there is absolutely no need for others.

The CHAIRMAN. Then, if there is no need for it, we will go down to the next question. You surely need a cemetery out there which ought to be set aside and ought to be made exempt from taxation. You ought to have as many cemeteries as you have different town sites.

ROBERT YELLOWTAIL. We would probably be agreeable to this whenever the agency or the grounds or places that have been abandoned for agency use are no longer required, then this town-site idea would work in pretty well, with that agency reserve.

The CHAIRMAN. You had better reserve your agency for future disposition of Congress. That is the reservation that should be made; it would enable Congress then to either allot it, sell it, or make a town site out of it, whichever the tribe wanted done.

ROBERT YELLOWTAIL. It would be hard for any individual or tribe to——

The CHAIRMAN. How many acres would you want set aside?

ROBERT YELLOWTAIL. Close to 320 acres.

The CHAIRMAN. Now, the oil provision as you have got it does not appeal to me as being drawn just right. You provide in the——

ROBERT YELLOWTAIL. What section is it?

The CHAIRMAN. Section 5. You provide that whatever cemeteries and town sites you set aside, or any reservations you make, ought to be exempt from taxation. That you have not provided here. I have got a memorandum of that.

Now, section 5, it seems to me, in view of the experience of the Indian Office, it would be better for you to follow the language of the Osage bill in reference to your leases, in reference to your reservation of oil and gas, because they have rules and regulations, except it is not provided for lease by tribal council; it is provided for lease by the department.

ROBERT YELLOWTAIL. We realize that the department—we can go into that by saying "under the existing law."

The CHAIRMAN. This is what I say here:

That the oil, gas, coal, or other minerals covered by the lands for the selection, division, and allotment for which provision is herein made are hereby reserved to the Crow Tribe for the period of 50 years from and after the date of the approval of this act, and leases for oil, gas, coal, and other minerals covered by selections and allotments herein provided for may be made under existing laws under such rules and regulations and conditions as the Secretary of the Interior may prescribe: *Provided*, That the patents issued to the members of the tribe for their selections and allotments shall contain a provision reserving all minerals for the benefit of the Crow Tribe: *Provided further*, That at the expiration of the 50 years all minerals upon or beneath the surface of any allotment shall become the property of the allottee or his heirs.

Now, you say "or his assigns." You are going to sell this. Any of this land that you sell, the people who buy are not going to pay you for the minerals, because of the 50-year reservation, yet under your provision you would give it to the man who buys at the end of 50 years in case it has not been developed. It seems to me that that is not fair at all; it ought to go to the heirs of the allottee.

ROBERT YELLOWTAIL. That would be all right.

The CHAIRMAN. Of course, I do not know how the other members of the committee will feel about the matter, but I am just making this suggestion to you.

Now, in section 6 you provide that the money be taken out of the Treasury of the United States. You have plenty of money in the Treasury, so why take it out of the Treasury and keep your double bookkeeping? That much would be paid out of the funds of the tribe, and then you do not have the double bookkeeping with separate accounts. Is that right, Mr. Meritt; or have they the money?

Mr. MERITT. Yes, sir; they have funds in the Treasury.

The CHAIRMAN. Then in addition to that you have the double bookkeeping. Think that over, will you?

ROBERT YELLOWTAIL. Yes, sir.

The CHAIRMAN. Now, in the next section it is provided—

SEC. 7. That any allotment, or part of allotment, provided for under this act, irrigable from any irrigation system now existing or hereafter constructed by the Government on the said reservation, shall bear its pro rata share, computed on a per acre basis, of the cost of constructing such system.

I have made this note on the side: Why not limit this to those who are benefited by the system? It does not seem to me—I may be mistaken about that, but from reading that over once it does not seem to me that it limits it to those who are benefited by the system, but makes the allotment liable whether it is benefited by the system or not. I wish you would think of that, Mr. Meritt, also.

Mr. MERITT. If you will read further down in that section, Mr. Chairman, I think that is covered.

The CHAIRMAN. Now, your 10-year reimbursement is absolutely too short. You ought to have that 20 years. On every reservation or every irrigation project we have in the United States we have had to extend the time. You will not get it through in 10 years, and you might as well get it first as last. Why not make it 20 years and be done with it?

ROBERT YELLOWTAIL. We have no objection to that. Make it more if you want to, and the more you make it the easier it will be to meet the payments.

The CHAIRMAN. I would make it 20 or 25 years at least, because you can not pay it in 10 years; white people are not paying it in 10 years, and if they can not do so how can an Indian pay it in 10 years?

ROBERT YELLOWTAIL. I suggest making it 25 years, then.

The CHAIRMAN. You think of that, you folks, before we go over the bill. Now, you provide over here in this section that that shall be foreclosed as a mortgage.

ROBERT YELLOWTAIL. We are following this right here. We took it out of Senator Walsh's bill; this bill here is, I might say, an amendment to Senator Walsh's bill.

The CHAIRMAN. As I understood it.

ROBERT YELLOWTAIL. We took it section by section and inserted our amendments and cut out the sections we thought we did not want. This is the exact language as used in the Walsh bill except as to the time limit.

The CHAIRMAN. You have left out some of the things that are in here that you have got to put in, it seems to me. You provide it shall be foreclosed as a mortgage. What about the poor helpless fellow that can not pay this and Mr. Agent, for some reason or another, thinks the man is not entitled to any further time and he forces a foreclosure. You are going to have him lose his property. I do not think that ought to be provided for in that way at all.

ROBERT YELLOWTAIL. Have you seen the last provision there?

The CHAIRMAN. I think it ought to be a lien upon his property when he sells it, but if he is going to still live there and make it his home, you ought not to authorize the department, it seems to me, to sell it under foreclosure.

ROBERT YELLOWTAIL. This is the same as in the bill that you had Mr. Nugent introduce, Mr. Meritt.

Mr. MERITT. I think we can strike out the words "and may be enforced by the Secretary of the Interior by foreclosure as a mortgage."

The CHAIRMAN. Does that not appeal to you, that if the fellow wants to live there he may be unable, and yet the agent might have some reason to be mad at him about something, and say, "Here is a worthless, good-for-nothing fellow; we will foreclose and get rid of him."

Mr. MERITT. As long as it makes a lien on the land I think that fully protects the Government.

Robert Yellowtail. You have not noticed this language, Senator:

That in no case shall any allottee be required to pay either construction, operation, or maintenance charges for such irrigation privileges, or any of them, until water has been actually delivered to his allotment and used by him, his heirs or assigns thereon, or until delivery of water thereto or thereon has been requested by him in writing.

We have inserted that provision to protect that very thing you speak of.

The Chairman. That does not protect him. What if he requests it and at the time he is all right? I have known Indians that were absolutely self-supporting, and for some reason or another said they were sick, and I have had no reason to believe but what they were sick, and yet I have heard the local agent say, "No; he is not sick; he is lazy," and simply force him to do things. I do not think he ought to be forced, and I think as long as he wants to live there it ought to be a lien until he sells it, to protect the Government.

Mr. Meritt. That is satisfactory; it is sufficient to protect the Government.

The Chairman. In line 6 I would say, " his heirs, tenants, or assigns "; probably the word " assigns " would include tenants. I doubt very much if it would or not; it is a broader term. It is an immaterial matter, but I noted it as I went over it.

Mr. Meritt. I would like to call your attention to that provision on page 7 beginning with line 2, which reads:

Provided, however, That in no case shall any allottee be required to pay either construction, operation, or maintenance charges for such irrigation privileges, or any of them, until water has been actually delivered to his allotment and used by him, his heirs or assigns thereon, or until delivery of water thereto or thereon has been requested by him in writing.

It will be a tract of land actually under irrigation, but because the Indian has not requested that land be irrigated, the land will not be subject to the construction charge.

Robert Yellowtail. Exactly; that is the thing we aim at.

Mr. Meritt. The irrigation people will naturally want all the land that is irrigated to bear its share of the construction charge, so as to bring down the construction charge to the lowest possible figure.

Robert Yellowtail. We had in mind a case over across the Big Horn River on a big flat there. Many of the allotments are over there, as you know. Quite a large majority of the Big Horn Indians' allotments are over there, and in case any Indian who has an allotment on this side of the water does not care to have his land across the river assessed for the construction of that private concern that might be built there at any time the authorization from the Department of the Interior is given to construct that big dam and that irrigation system that they are planning to build, anybody that wants to be free of assessments for the construction charge, if he is on that ditch, until he felt properly able financially to meet these dues, he ought to be free to do that. With that idea in mind we inserted that provision.

The Chairman. Is it a private concern?

Robert Yellowtail. Yes, sir.

The Chairman. Well, they could not force an Indian.

Robert Yellowtail. We do not know whether it is private now, but a big concern planned to take that over.

The Chairman. Of course you built all that you have now out of your own funds.

Robert Yellowtail. Yes, sir; but we would not build any more on the Big Horn, because it would take several times more than they have to build it.

The Chairman. If it is a private concern, they will do as they do in other private concerns; you will not be required to pay for water until you are connected up.

Robert Yellowtail. That is the suggestion he made a while ago. They would naturally want everything underneath it to help.

The Chairman. You could change that; you could reword that to make it apply to existing projects that have been built by Indian funds to be reimbursed upon sale of the property or upon use, etc., and then you could provide that any new projects or property should not be required to pay until they were connected. I do not think there would be anyhow if it is a private proposition, because private people could not force you to use it.

Robert Yellowtail. We do not know whether it is going to be private or not.

The Chairman. It is one hundred to one that you people would not build any more.

Robert Yellowtail. No, sir; if we build any, it would be simply for protection.

Mr. Asbury. Mr. Chairman, there is another important feature to that clause. If the ditch was built, say, covering 2,000 acres, and a thousand of that did not elect to use the water, and it went on several years, in the meantime the water might all be appropriated and they would lose their water right to that construction.

The Chairman. Yes; that has got to be looked after.

Mr. Asbury. That condition is approaching on our smaller streams; on the Little Horn and Lodgegrass and smaller streams, and the time is approaching when the water will all be appropriated.

Robert Yellowtail. Then it takes mutual consent of the Indians upon that project. If you give mutual consent, or tribal consent, naturally everybody would abide by the decision of those underneath.

The Chairman. You people talk that over and see if we can not arrange something satisfactory. In this connection—I did not intend to take it up now—I will say that I have been told that in these leases you have at the present time covering irrigated and nonirrigated land, that they are forcing those Indians to lease. A man will have a tract of land in the middle of a big tract that is covered by the lease, and now they are forcing that fellow on the inside to lease to them, or they are fencing him out. I did not bring it to your attention, but I brought it to the attention of the commissioner and he said he would look into it. If that is true it would be an outrage and ought not to be permitted. No man ought to be forced to lease his land unless he wants to lease it. My attention was brought to a case yesterday—and I am going to ask Mr. Sloan to tell you and the committee about it— one man was forced to lease his property and he was getting virtually nothing out of it, this year. Last year he got $700 for his grass land. Now, those things discourage members of the tribe and they ought not to be permitted for a minute. A man ought not to be forced to lease unless he wants to, unless he has some land under an irrigation project that he is allowing to go to waste.

Mr. MERITT. I do not think there is anything in that. I do not think there is any one who would force an Indian to lease to Mr. Campbell.

The CHAIRMAN. My attention has been called to two or three cases by letter, and I brought one to the attention of the department, and then I talked with Mr. Sloan yesterday, who has just been up there and whom I have known for a good many years, and I was asking him about this and he told me about this one man. I want you to consider that, because I want that taken up when the bill is acted upon.

Now, as to section 9, you say:

SEC. 9. That any unallotted lands on the Crow Reservation chiefly valuable for the development of water power shall be reserved from allotment or other disposition hereunder, for the benefit of the Crow Tribe of Indians, and be held subject to such sale, lease, or other disposition as the tribe may, with the approval of Congress, hereafter make thereof.

If you are going to lease it, why do you want to come to Congress with a lease? Why not make that lease subject to the approval of the department? You know how hard it is to get a bill through Congress. It might get through and it might not get through; it might be a year or two years.

ROBERT YELLOWTAIL. In all probability the leasing feature may never materialize, but we are anticipating a probable sale; a sale, or probably a water site.

The CHAIRMAN. Why do you not reserve that for future disposition of the tribe through Congress?

ROBERT YELLOWTAIL. We have.

The CHAIRMAN. But you have the other provision in there, and then you provide that the leases may be made with the consent of the tribal council and the approval of the Secretary of the Interior.

Mr. MERITT. I have made a note of that, and the amendment I have suggested is disposition as the tribe may agree, with the approval of the Secretary of the Interior, and subject to such laws as Congress may hereafter enact.

There is pending before Congress now the power-leasing bill, and that bill will take care of the power sites on the reservation, and the proceeds will go to the Indians. If that bill is amended as I have suggested, the Secretary may supervise that leasing and the Indians will be protected.

ROBERT YELLOWTAIL. I will tell you, Mr. Meritt, what you have done beforehand when it comes to the disposition of our water-power sites. We have an opinion by this man Cooper, who was working on the Panama Canal, who pronounced it to be one of the best in the United States. Nobody who knows anything about power development would fail to agree with that, I guess. It is a mighty big project, and, of course, it represents quite a tribal asset to us. We, of course, are desirous of exercising a voice in the disposition of that matter, and having that idea in view we worded this as it is worded here so we might have, when Congress acts, naturally a chance to express our opinion, and we do not want to lose that right; that is a fundamental right that all American people demand is theirs all the time, and if there is anything said about the disposition of the tribal lands or tribal assets we want to be right here to say what we have to say, whether they listen to us or not.

Mr. MERITT. Under this amendment of mine the tribe will have a voice in the disposition.

ROBERT YELLOWTAIL. You will see to that?

The CHAIRMAN. Yes. Now, as to your request to send your case to the Court of Claims, it seems to me, in line 25, you should add "all claims of whatever nature." You say, "all claims," and if you add "of whatever nature," you might possibly have some disposition of it. I think that is the usual language, is it not, Mr. Meritt?

Mr. MERITT. Yes, sir.

The CHAIRMAN. Now, further over there, the question of your presenting your petition verified by an attorney. That has got to be fought out by the entire committee, so there is no use of saying anything about that at this time.

You have no provision in here, it seems to me, about the segregation of funds, and I drew this amendment as I went along:

That all the funds of the Crow Tribe of Indians and all moneys now due or that may be found to be due to said Crow Tribe of Indians from any source, and all moneys that may be received as reimbursements for tribal moneys expended for the establishment and maintenance of the irrigation system or systems on the Crow Reservation, and all moneys found to be due to the said Crow Tribe of Indians on claims against the United States, after all expenses for which the tribe may be liable, shall be segregated as soon as practicable after the passage of this act and placed to the credit of the individual members of said Crow Tribe on a pro rata division among the members of said tribe, as shown by the authorized roll of membership as herein provided for, or to their heirs as hereinafter provided, said credit to draw interest as now authorized by law, and the interest that may accrue thereon shall be paid quarterly to the members entitled thereto, except in cases of minors, in which case the interest shall be paid quarterly to the parents until said minors arrive at the age of 21 years: *Provided*, That if the Commissioner of Indian Affairs becomes satisfied that the interest of any minor is being misused or squandered he may withhold the payment of such interest and use the same for the best interest of any such minor: *Provided further*, That interest of minors whose parents are deceased shall be paid to their legal guardians.

You have absolutely, as I recollect it, no clause on that subject at all. It seems to me you need something on that, and I drew that up as a suggestion.

ROBERT YELLOWTAIL. We are not objecting to it.

The CHAIRMAN. It is not a question of objecting. I am just suggesting it to you. Take that, anyhow, as a suggestion. There is no harm in being very careful about these things. How about the irrigated lands that have been sold? What is your plan on that? What do they do now? Do they pay for the irrigation?

Mr. MERITT. They pay the Indian for the land and assume the obligation to pay the construction charge.

The CHAIRMAN. Is that provided for by rules and regulations, or is there some existing law upon the subject? There ought to be some provision, it seems to me, in this bill providing for that, that irrigated lands or lands within a project heretofore sold shall pay its pro rata share of the cost of construction, and the maintenance shall be paid by the purchaser.

Mr. MERITT. I think that should be made perfectly clear.

The CHAIRMAN. There is no question about it, and if you will make a memorandum of that to be considered by your people, I would like to have you do it. Now, you provide in this bill that you shall have a patent in fee, and yet you provide over in the last of your bill that each Indian shall have a homestead of 640 acres, and that that shall be exempt for how many years?

Robert Yellowtail. Twenty-five years.

The Chairman. Twenty-five years, or is it 50 years?

Mr. Meritt. Twenty-five years.

The Chairman. Twenty-five years. The two are inconsistent. If you get a patent in fee, that settles it. The Indian can do as he pleases with the land; he can sell it to-morrow if he wants to. Now, you will have to draw another provision, it seems to me, covering that question. I sent this bill to each member of the committee, and several of them have spoken to me about the size of that homestead. The general impression, as I gather it from the committee, is that the homestead ought to be limited to 40 acres of irrigated lands, 160 acres of farming land, and 320 acres of grazing land. This came to me from two members of the committee yesterday. I want you to think about that.

Robert Yellowtail. Of course, there is this question that will arise, and I will suggest it. They assume that every member of the committee probably is under an irrigation project, which is false to begin with. Many are located upon springs in the hills, and it is a question of grazing land with them. The 40-acre rule can not apply to all of them, because the projects are not large enough.

The Chairman. That is true; but you can get the value out of them. If I was drawing this bill—I will be very frank with you—I would divide the land into three classes—irrigation, farming, and grazing. Then I would take your other lands, your mountain lands, which I want to ask you about later, and I would put that in a separate division by itself. Then I would give to each Indian his pro rata share of that land. If he had irrigated land, I would give him less farming and less grazing. If he had farming land, I would give him more than I did the irrigated land; and if he wanted pasture, I would give him more pasture land. If it was all grazing land, I would give him more. Now, if you do that, you will give to each member of the tribe his fair share of the property; but if you give each a homestead of 640 acres and do not count your irrigation, you are going to give an Indian 40 acres who happens to be lucky enough and far enough advanced to settle down where he gets irrigation; you are going to give him 40 acres worth $100 an acre, and then you are going to give him land worth $1.25 an acre, enough to make up the balance, while the poor fellow out here in the hills is going to get land which is only worth about $1.25 or $2 an acre. I do not know anything about the values; I am using these to illustrate. That is not fair to the members of the tribe.

Robert Yellowtail. The irrigation projects are already allotted underneath; there is hardly an acre there.

The Chairman. You have them allotted?

Robert Yellowtail. They are already allotted. Now, what are you going to do?

The Chairman. That is the point. They are already allotted. If they are not allotted, allot the balance of them so as to give you men out on the hills and in the farming land and grazing land an allotment equivalent to the allotment of the fellow down there with his irrigation land. When you have equalized that then divide the balance among them. We have had a number of reservations where Indians—where we had to divide the land into farming and grazing, 800 acres of grazing land—400 acres of grazing land to be given to a member of the tribe in Oklahoma and 160 acres of farming land.

Robert Yellowtail. You would have the greatest rumpus you have ever heard of if you adopt your plan. In the aggregate some would have probably 300 acres and some 700 acres, because they are on the hills. A proposition of that sort would never be agreeable to the tribe as a whole.

The Chairman. Why do they not want each man to have his proportionate share?

Robert Yellowtail. Yes; that is fair enough all right.

The Chairman. It is the other fellow that is farther advanced, and you want to take away from the fellow who has nothing.

Robert Yellowtail. Of course I do not know what this man or that man wants to do; they have agreed to prorate the thing with regard to acreage as against values.

The Chairman. What do you mean? Take so many acres?

Robert Yellowtail. So many acres; of course those that are allotted are allotted already; the projects you speak of are fully alloted underneath with the exception of an occasional selection here and there. Those that are unfortunate enough to be outside of the irrigation project would simply, under the terms of this bill——

The Chairman. Is it your idea to give these men who have their selections down here in the irrigated country, and have—how many acres have they got, 40?

Robert Yellowtail. It depends on how much is underneath there.

The Chairman. How many acres are usually allotted to the Indians there?

Robert Yellowtail. Forty.

The Chairman. Forty acres of irrigated land? Now, is it your idea to give him 40 acres and then give him out on the other part of the reservation enough to bring him up to 640 acres, or give him his pro rata share regardless of that?

Robert Yellowtail. Absolutely.

The Chairman. And then give some other fellow who has no irrigated land a sufficient number of acres?

Robert Yellowtail. Yes, sir; I am one of those fellows up in the hills too. It is not my idea, Senator Curtis; it is the vote of the council to divide with regard to acreage as against values.

The Chairman. Was the question presented to them?

Robert Yellowtail. Which question?

The Chairman. The question of the unfairness of it, how much advantage one Indian would have over another.

Robert Yellowtail. That feature we have never discussed. We are discussing it here. Even if we discussed that feature, they would contend that they have a right to have an equal acreage when the allotment was completed and the rest would agree with them. The committee would have to do that, of course, if they had the power to do it, against the vote of the tribe, because they would not get the consent of the tribe to do it.

The CHAIRMAN. Of course the committee has the power to do it; what we want to do is what is best for the tribe, if the thing was properly presented to the tribe, they would want it themselves. You take the Cherokees in Oklahoma—

Mr. FRANK YARLOTT. I think Senator Curtis's suggestion is a very good one. It is a question of equal division of the land, and it would be fair, as you have stated here, but the details have not been gone into as to just how that should be done. They wanted all the land allotted equally.

The CHAIRMAN. That is, dividing it in acres?

Mr. YARLOTT. Yes.

The CHAIRMAN. We can take that up later; we can not take any action this morning.

Now, I want to talk to you a minute about another matter. You make no provision for the reservation of this mountain land. I understood you to say to me the other day that the object of the tribe was to preserve the mountain land. Have you got it preserved there? I do not find it anywhere. Any reservation you want to make ought to be a specific reservation; it ought to be in the bill, just the same as reserving anything else.

Mr. MERITT. They ought not to be required to make a survey.

The CHAIRMAN. That is throwing money away and is a waste of time. What you ought to do, is to draw one section, reserving these mountain sections, describing them and providing that those lands at this time should not be surveyed, but retained as tribal property to be used as a common herding ground, or whatever you want to do with it; it ought to be used in common for the benefit of the tribe.

ROBERT YELLOWTAIL. We left that out. We had it in another section that we wanted to insert. We wanted to save time and give it to Senator Walsh.

The CHAIRMAN. The trouble is you are not saving much time.

ROBERT YELLOWTAIL. We have been here for two weeks and this is the first opportunity we have had to come before the committee, and we want to get this thing started.

The CHAIRMAN. Your bill was not introduced until last week.

ROBERT YELLOWTAIL. Senator Walsh, I understand, said that he was interested in the oil leasing bill and preferred to wait until that was disposed of.

The CHAIRMAN. We will not have any discussion of that, Robert. Now, I do not like the disposition you have made here of your tribal herd. Of course I think the herd ought to be disposed of under such plan as is satisfactory to the majority of the members of the tribe, but when you dispose of the tribal herd, you have got to, it seems to me, protect the fellow who can not protect himself. You provide for a sale; you say nothing about whether the market is good or bad; and you provide for dividing the money among the incompetents. Now, if you are going to reserve the mountain lands as a common herding ground, or as common property—is it grass land there at all?

ROBERT YELLOWTAIL. No. It is probably able to carry 5,000 head during the summer. Mr. Heindrick, who has been using it for the past 25 years, has put that many there.

The CHAIRMAN. Why would it not be the better plan to save the cattle of the incompetents and put them in that section and hold them until the Indians became so they could take care of them themselves, and as they could take care of them, turn them over to them on their places with a provision that they could not be sold. They can not be sold now under the law, but I think there ought to be a provision put in this bill that they should be branded and they should be retained and not sold, not mortgaged and not disposed of. As I say, they can not be now, but for safety's sake, I put a provision in the bill with reference to those cattle.

Mr. MERITT. Under that bill they propose to prorate the tribal herd?

The CHAIRMAN. They want to sell it?

Mr. MERITT. On that point I want to say, after talking with the commissioner, he is very much opposed to the prorating of this tribal herd at this time.

The CHAIRMAN. I think the competents ought to have their share if they want it.

Mr. MERITT. He is perfectly willing that the competent Indians shall withdraw their prorata share, but we believe, after considering this Crow question very carefully, that the land between the two rivers should be reserved at the present time—the district known as the Flatiron district—and that the tribal herd should not be prorated now, but only the competent Indians should be permitted to take their prorata share of the tribal herd.

The CHAIRMAN. You are going to have some full bloods there who are designated as incompetents, and it seems to me they would take just as good care of their cattle as the competents.

Mr. MERITT. If they are competent to take care of the cattle, we will permit them to take their share.

The CHAIRMAN. If you have any Indians who are classed as incompetent, who are capable of taking care of their cattle, you are to turn them over to them.

Mr. MERITT. We will be glad to do that. Any Indian who is capable of taking care of his prorata share——

The CHAIRMAN. Why can not you draw a provision to the effect that those who have been found to be competent shall be given their share and those that are classed as incompetent that the cattle shall be reserved or held, but that any Indian classed as incompetent who has demonstrated that he has ability to take care of cattle, etc., shall have his share turned over to him with the provision in the bill that they shall not be mortgaged or sold or disposed of in any way?

Mr. MERITT. That will be entirely agreeable to us.

The CHAIRMAN. Except, I think—I do not know how you people feel about it, but I have been awfully disappointed that Indians on the reservation were permitted to go hungry in the wintertime when they had a lot of cattle; I think your agent should see to it for those people who are unable to take care of themselves that cattle are killed every so often and the meat distributed among those people who are entitled to it. You surely have some cattle of that kind which you could kill. This has just occurred to me, and I do not care especially about it.

ROBERT YELLOWTAIL. We want to be heard on that issue.

The CHAIRMAN. You are going to be heard on all of these questions, but I am talking to you about things I see and I am going to make a suggestion when I get through with this. Now, I am very strongly in favor of a proposition of letting you people sell a certain amount of your land—I mean letting the competents dispose of their lands the way they please, but I am for the incompetents; if they are land poor, let some of their lands be sold for their benefit on 20 or 25 years' time, with preference given to those soldiers. I think it would be a wonderful thing for you. It will get you a good, honest class of people on the reservation. It gives them a chance, and it gives these incompetent Indians a little income every year for 25 or 30 years, and at the end of 25 or 30 years they could pay for it. They could make small payments after the first 2 or 3 years, say the first 2 years, without any pay, and make them pay interest for the first 2 years, and then make them begin to divide up something like we did the Kaw proposition. The result there was you provided for a division of their money in 10 years. You had no complaint, no appeal; you gave them one-tenth every year for 10 years, and you had no trouble about it.

Mr. MERITT. No, sir.

The CHAIRMAN. Now, if you make this for 20 years, you could make the payments at such times in the fall as would help the Indians and have the payments so that the Indians would know they would get so much in the spring, which would help in buying what he wanted for his planting, and in the fall give him something to spend for the winter. It would help the soldier or any other man— I would only sell it to bona fide purchasers; I would not sell a foot of it to a speculator.

ROBERT YELLOWTAIL. We have no way of determining that.

The CHAIRMAN. If a man buys more than a certain limit, you can forfeit his deed; you can have that provision in the deed. The deed can be arranged if you want to do it. Now, if you do not, you are going to sell it under the existing plan; it will be sold for cash and the money will be paid into the Treasury and the Indians will get just the same interest, probably not so much interest, probably he will get 4 per cent, or whatever you agree in the bill. The other way, he will probably pay you 5 per cent, and when it is paid it is paid in a lump sum and it is gone overnight; the other way, the Indian has 25 years or 20 years in which to prepare himself, and in the meantime his children are being better prepared; they are having this experience of handling this money; the first year they will probably squander all of it right away and the next year they will save it. I know that is what they did down in Oklahoma. They got so they knew when this money was coming in and they would arrange with that and what they had, and they got along very nicely. There was absolutely no complaint about it. The only regret I had was we did not extend it over a 20-year period.

Now, then, you have this other proposition which I think you ought to consider, and I do not know whether the department agrees with me or not. You have out there—you had a number of years ago, and I do not see anyone here representing those people—you had a number of Indians that were allotted, given certain certificates of allotment, and some of them were given patents which were canceled. I do not know why the department canceled them. I suppose they thought they had good reason for it. I do not think the department has the right to cancel any of those patents.

Robert Yellowtail. They were given permission, I think, to relinquish on that portion.

The Chairman. Did they relinquish voluntarily, or were they forced to do so? Anyhow, there ought to be a provision in this bill protecting their interests if they were forced out. I do not know; I have not had any letters from any of them. While, I think, when I was in Congress before, I had a letter from one of the women and took it up with your department when I was in the Senate six or eight years ago. She had been given the patent and sent the patent to me and I sent it to the office. Her patent had been canceled, and she had been given another allotment, as she said, over her protest, and on the diminishing reservation.

Now, I do not think a provision in this bill is necessary, because I think those people can go to the courts now, if the statute of limitations has not run; but I am going to suggest it for such action as the committee thinks proper, and I would like to have the department consider it. I think there ought to be a provision protecting their interests, letting them go to the courts if they want to.

Now, another thing. It seems to me in this bill that you have taken the position really—I would not suggest it if I was a member of the tribe. You have arranged for a commission, one member of your tribe, one a citizen of Montana, and your agent. Now, if I was a member of that tribe and was going to divide that land, I would have a majority of that committee members of my tribe. You have perfectly competent men there. You remember in Oklahoma we had one tribe that you did not have an outsider on, except the agent, and there was not a contest which came to your office. You remember that?

Mr. Meritt. Yes.

The Chairman. Those Indians can better settle their own little controversies about allotments than any white man who does not know anything about their conditions; the white man does not know the relationships; he simply goes there and sees this tract of land allotted, and that tract of land, and he does not know anything about the relationship; he does not know whether the man is a second cousin to somebody else or not.

These members do know all of that and they can settle this. If I was going to draw this bill, I would put a majority of that allotting committee members of the tribe; I would make three members of the tribe allotting commissioners, and I would put the agent, and if they wanted one outside citizen, I would put him on, too. I would give a majority of that commission to the tribe itself, making everything subject, of course, to the approval of the department, so if any fraud was perpetrated you could correct it.

Mr. Meritt. That is exactly what we have done. We have one from the tribe itself and one a citizen of the State of Montana.

The Chairman. Do you mean he is to be an Indian?

Robert Yellowtail. That is the idea we have in mind.

Mr. Meritt. Who shall be an enrolled Crow Indian?

Robert Yellowtail. One a citizen of the State of Montana. We have lots of them on the reservation who are citizens of the State of Montana and enrolled members of the tribe, too.

The Chairman. Of course you do not say that. If you made it two and one it would be all right, but you ought to have a majority of your tribe on that commission. There is no question about that;

it is your property; it belongs to the tribe, and that property ought to be divided for the best interests of the tribe, and I would change that provision and make it, if you want him, that an enrolled member of the tribe, who is a citizen of Montana, an enrolled member of the tribe, and if it is satisfactory to the other members of the committee, so far as I am concerned, it is satisfactory.

Robert Yellowtail. One commissioner shall be a legal citizen of the State of Montana.

The Chairman. Yes; say an enrolled member of the tribe. I think you are wise in having a small commission, unless you happen to be unfortunate in selecting new men on there that might not be working in harmony.

Now, I have asked a good many questions here. I have some others, but I have a memorandum of them, and I want to go over to the Capitol at 12, and I wish you would do this: I wish you would take these suggestions that I have made; take this bill; take the old Department bill, and you and your people get down together and sit down and see if you can not agree upon some amendments, and then I will ask Mr. Walsh and other members of the committee about appointing a subcommittee, and I will ask that subcommittee to sit with you folks, members of your tribe, and the Commissioner and Superintendent and see if we can not work out a bill that will be satisfactory. I want to say the members of the committee desire to protect the interests of the Crow tribe of Indians; the members of the committee wish to protect those fellows who can not protect themselves out there. You and a few others can take care of yourselves.

Robert Yellowtail. You will see no attempt on my part and the part of a few others to deprive these fellows of any rights.

The Chairman. I have not suggested that.

Robert Yellowtail. If there is anything between them and us, I do not care who it is, they will not get away with it.

The Chairman. I did not make that suggestion to reflect on anybody, but stated that to let you know how the members of the committee feel. They want to protect the Indians who can not protect themselves, and they want to help you get up that kind of bill.

Mr. Meritt. Mr. Chairman, there is one provision in this bill that is very objectionable to the Commissioner, and that is in relation to the employment of an attorney.

The Chairman. That—I guess we will have to leave that out. The committee is divided on that question, and we will have to leave that out and fight it out in the committee, and I hope the department will draw its amendment, and then we will put the question squarely. We have it in the case of the Flatheads; we have it in five or six cases, and we have to determine by the committee what procedure we will have. I think you suggested he would be employed and approved under section so and so of the statute.

Mr. Meritt. If the bill were amended by putting after the word "claim," in line 13, page 18, "with the approval of the Commissioner of Indian Affairs and the Secretary of the Interior as required by existing law."

The Chairman. Yes; or you can say, "as required by existing law," without putting that in there. That will have to be fought out by the full committee, and there is no use of our wasting time on it here.

If there is nothing else, I will notify you people.

Robert Yellowtail. That will be all right with us.

The Chairman. I thank you for coming here and remaining this morning and listening to one member of the committee, but I thought we could save time if these matters could be brought to your attention. A lot of this has been offhand, and I might have other things when we meet again. I would suggest that you take it down and have an appointment with the Commissioner, and take these three or four bills and see how much you can vamp out and agree upon among yourselves. There will be other suggestions probably made when other members of the committee come here. I do not know but what we will have your bill slashed then. If you wish I will appoint a subcommittee to go over the bill with you and see if you can not get something nearly perfect, and then I will ask for a full committee and urge them to be here.

Robert Yellowtail. After we meet, probably we will have something to submit that will be final.

Mr. Meritt. I think probably we might be able to get together on these matters.

(Thereupon, at 12 o'clock m., the committee adjourned subject to the call of the chairman.)

×

Printed by Libri Plureos GmbH in Hamburg,
Germany